anonymous.

anisah a. ali

Anonymous
By Anisah A. Ali

Book design by Kyle Lane
Illustrations by Deun Ivory

• • •

www.anisahali.com

Table of Contents

Prose

poetry

Intro

to the souls who believe
they are alone in
their struggle:
you are not alone.
there are souls
wandering this earth
who run up against
trials every day;
merge with me.
be one with them.

to the voices that
have been dipped
in silence: speak.
find your voice.
it's searching for you.

to the mistakes:
you are appreciated.
without you
we would never be
forced to grow up.

to the experiences:
the ones that make
life worth it,
the ones that make
you question your
very existence.

to love:
i believe in you.
i feel you in my
movements, my heart,
my spirit.
i vow to project and
protect you
from the world.

to hurt, to pain:
i still feel you.
i've accepted that you
may forever be
a part of me.
i have accepted that
no matter how much
i try to write you off or
express you out of me,
you are me.
you are the reason
i am who i am and
i am okay with you
finding comfort in me.

to self, i've learned to
honor you. i've learned
to respect and protect
your heart. i've
learned to be sensitive
and not so hard on you.
i've learned that there

is beauty and life
in your mistakes.
above all, i've learned
to love you.

this is for you.

to the souls who have
remained anonymous,
this is for you.
this is for all of you.
this is for us.

"for most of history, anonymous was a woman."
virginia woolf

Just Like You

what do you want to be
when you grow up?

i want to be just like my papa.

second grade,
career day.
i had my life
figured out.
they told me it
was nice that i
wanted to
be like you.

nice was the word
they used.

as if i wanted to
be like you
out of kindness
or to make you
feel better about
being who you were.

they said i had to
pick something more
realistic.

hesitation left
lumps in their

throats:
how do you tell
  a second grader
she couldn't be
whoever or
  whatever she
wanted to be.

well, what does that
look like? being like
your father?

it looked like
  being everything
i loved about you:
the supernatural
  ability to escape
the world within
  the pages of a book.
falling in love with
  the characters,
the wisdom.
  navigating
through other
  worlds,
enhancing my
imagination.

it looked like
being a writer:

creating an outlet
to dispense
sadness and hurt
and regret.
that's what being
like my papa
looked like.

maybe not even
that was enough.

being like you had to
be more than
good literature and
creating.

but, i wasn't ready
wasn't willing
to be like the
rest of you.

i remember being
in the second grade,
eyes bright, as i
imagined you being
more than you were:

perfect.

Living Without Fear

fear is not a trait
we are born with
but one that is learned.

remember being a child:
your life void of
fear and full of existing
within vulnerable spaces,
climbing to the top of
monkey bars and standing tall.
the world at your feet.
speaking your every
thought into existence,
a lack of fear for
what others thought,
a lack of care for
being judged.

when did we lose that power?
when did we lose the ability
to be vulnerable?
the ability to be daring?

can we get it back?

Things My Father Taught Me

1. egos must be stroked.
2. not tamed.
3. find someone to spend your life with who will adhere to rule one.
4. love with limitations.
5. chaos solves problems.
6. or it doesn't.
7. you apologize later.
8. or you don't.
9. love with expectations.
10. or not at all.
11. pile on a grudge or two.
12. relationships are a business deal.
13. it's easier to abandon people you share DNA with.
14. forgiveness is a treasure.
15. never give it away.

in my mother's house
there was a painting
that sat on the wall
like the house was
structured around it.

in the painting,
sat a little girl.
plaits disoriented
across her head.

she sat slouched
in a seat that
stood proud in the
corner of the house
grandma and grandpa
raised their children in.
the house that their love
grew up in.
the house where holidays and
collard greens and
memories brewed in.

her pink dress with a
world of frills peeking
from below carried
two or three wrinkles.
i knew that's not how
it looked when mama

dressed her that morning.

this little girl was a rich
dark chocolate,
i wanted to be her.

i wanted to be the girl
who caught wrinkles
in her dress.
i wanted to be the girl
who knew she'd get in
trouble for "acting like
a boy" in her sunday's
best but did it anyway.

i wanted to be the girl...
the girl in the painting that
stood proud on the wall of
my mother's house.

Childhood

you and i were
bundles full
  of joy.

daddy, you raised me.
  food satisfied our
bellies and
  the years you carried of
growing and learning
  and loving satisfied
even bigger appetites.

you checked under
  our bed for monsters
you knew were
  never there
and shared
  bowls of cereal
after midnight,
when my sister
  and i couldn't
rest our eyes.

you never read
us bedtime stories.
you made them up.
  you made us laugh
when you thought
we hadn't laughed
  in a while.

you were the reason
for our face-
cracking smiles.

you would drive
us to school every
morning and turn the
radio down low so
we could act out our
own radio show.

we would always
have dinner together.
and you would want
to know every detail
of our day, you wanted
to know if we smelled
any flowers on
our way home
from school or if
we counted
how many rocks
from the playground
hid in our shoe.

you and i were
parallel.

our lives ran
simultaneously
alongside one
another.

only i'm not sure
where they crossed
or where our
  paths got lost.

Defined As...

father: noun: *a male parent*

the first man to show you how
to be treated
a male ancestor

to be loved
parental protector
to be respected.
provider

to be honored.

originated or established something

my father:

my first heartbreak.

Once Upon A Time

i needed you to be
  the hero.
the fairy tales i
  read never wrote
a hero who
  saved themselves
from them self.

i wanted you to be
  prince charming;
i pictured you as
  such when we
danced to the music
  in our heads
in the living room.
  mama watching in
the corner,
  a light flashing
from her camera,
freezing the memory.

i wished for you
  to get rid of
the monsters;
  not become one.

i wrote this story
  out late nights,
stored it in the
  top bunk of

my thoughts
where i knew no
one could ever try
to change it.

i looked out of
my window
each night,
mistaking airplanes
for shooting stars,
making wishes on
them anyway.

i picked dandelions
that had not yet
bloomed into
flowers that
resembled
the sunshine.
i figured with
magic like that,
it could make
my wishes come
true.

i have never trusted
a dandelion the same,
maybe it gave up
on me
every time i
spoke your name.

daddy stormed through
my bedroom,
destructive in a space
that was never
his own.

he bullied my
belongings,
throwing them
to the floor,
shoving them around.
his enrage becoming
an outrage.

he found skeletons
that i buried in the
back of my closet
under last week's
underwear,
this month's laundry,
yesterday's lunch and
tomorrow's homework.

he spilled my skeletons
out in front of me.

after he created a mess,
brought the storm in
because someone

rained on his day,
he announced:
now you stay in here until
it's all cleaned up.

Never Mistake the Two

mistakes became
claustrophobic,
there was very
little space for them.
you injected me with
an overdose of fear
yet the label read love.

there was no way
that this could be love.

Anger

it takes you on a journey you may not
be prepared for. opens doors you wished
to remain closed. produces energy that pollutes
your surroundings. be careful how you
distribute it and the extremes you may
allow it to take you.

it took many
moons for me
to believe
in myself.
it was something
i had to teach
myself how to do.

i had to understand
what it meant to
be comfortable with
showing up in every
room as myself,
i had to be comfortable
with who i was,
with who i became.

i had to be confident
within the spaces i chose
to occupy with an
awareness that i
deserved to be
within those spaces.

i had to claw away
at the hate that
grew around my
soul to find love
and learn how to
give it to myself.

i still have moments
when i lack the
belief and love
and confidence
in myself.
it is all a part of
the process.
there is no final
destination.

there is no right or
perfect way to
love yourself.
it is all a journey.
always growing and
forever changing.

On the Possibilities of Fixing a Broken Wing

she was like a
butterfly with
a fractured wing:
not easily
broken.

for all things
with a slight
frailty obtain
the possibility
of being repaired.

one day, afforded
the ability
to fly again.

What 13-Year-Old Girls Learn

1. your body is a country: explored yet beautiful. abused yet sacred. taken advantage of.
2. not respected.
3. the first boy who touches you, doesn't love you.
4. boys smell like bodies tumbling in the grass under burning sun rays and dirt stained jeans and sweat.
5. your breasts will swell.
6. boys will try to touch them.
7. when he tells you not to tell anyone, you don't.
8. laying on your back gives you views of ceilings in your great grandmother's house that resemble rainbows in star-lit skies.
9. have you ever seen a rainbow at night?
10. your grandfather's footsteps in hallways lined with sepia photos saves you from being damaged any further; he releases his body weight when he hears them.
11. but the destruction is already done.
12. having your period makes you a woman.
13. you are wrecked and damaged and tainted.

What 13-Year-Old Girls Should Learn

1. your body is sacred.
2. when he tells you not to tell, you tell anyway.
3. when he has you pinned down to the ground, you scream until you can no longer feel his body weight.
4. boys smell like grass stained jeans and sweat; don't let them near you.
5. don't let them touch you.
6. punch them in the face when they try.
7. you're stronger than them.
8. you are beautiful and magical.
9. have you ever seen a rainbow at night?
10. don't try to grow up too fast. hold on to being a little girl.
11. it doesn't last forever.
12. don't be afraid or ashamed of your womb shedding. celebrate it. it means your body works; it knows how to communicate with you.
13. you are delicate and innocent and lovely.

After the Rainfall

from the experiences
that were meant to
leave her shattered,
she bloomed.
she carried the aroma
of fresh rainfall and
double rainbows.

Trial

it was about the
mistakes i made and
the fucked up person
i became. it had
nothing to do with
the way i was raised.
if we looked at it that way,
it would be a
reflection of you.

the goal that made
it on the top of
my list was to please
one person.
one person out
of billions.

but no one else
mattered but you.

what mattered was
clearing my name
from the crime,
convincing you,
the one who became
the judge and the jury,
that i did my time.

i allowed you to

matter for too long.
it extracted a chunk
from my life.
a piece of my life
that i would
never get back.

i used to live
life to please you:

the un-pleasable.

she wore lonely well
like men doused in scents
of cheap alcohol, well.
like heels that made
your feet callous and
a self-esteem below
soles, well.

happiness
would never fit her.

happiness was sunday
suits and dresses pushed
in the back of closets
with skeletons.

happiness was
a baby's first laugh.

happiness was walking
miles on clouds with
no real destination
other than a front seat
to watch the moon rise.

happiness would never
look good on her;
it would never fit a
woman with hips like hers.

it would never bring
out the sorrow that
filled her eyes.
it would never make
the corners of her
lips lift like cotton
candy sunrises.

happiness would
never look good on
her, it would never fit.

Solar Complex

the sun bends
towards you
and illuminates
your presence.
how is it that
you demand
the attention
of one of the
most radiant
goddesses of the
galaxy and you
never realized:
you are perfection.

Natural Disaster

you were
made from
earthquakes and
hurricanes:
a sudden release
of toxic energy.
you were a
'rapidly rotating
storm system.'
you shook up
worlds. you
caused chaos.

then, in the end,
you were silent.
you watched as
lost and damaged
souls scrambled
to collect the
pieces of their
lives and put them
back together again.

daddy,
you were full of
justifications.
full of 'i did it
because i can' and
'i did it because

you hurt me ' and
i did it because,
well, because....

you were this
broken thing.
broken pieces
that were never
properly rearranged.
you hated the way
your brokenness
resided on your body.
you hated the way
it ran rampant and
destroyed and
metastasized.
you despised the
broken parts of
you so much,
you needed everyone
else to be broken.

so you broke us.

From a Cabin in the Woods

the beautiful thing
about this journey is
it's yours.

this journey is yours
to run through dark
forests into branches
of mistakes.

this journey is yours
to blossom a bouquet
of lessons, allowing
disbelievers to witness
the magic they
fail to see in you.

this journey is
yours to engrave a
legacy in the hearts of
every tree you touch,
like lovers chisel their
initials in confidence
that no matter what
tries to tear them down,
this imprint means
forever and always.

Lessons from 16

you aren't perfect.
i'm not sure you
ever were.

you loved the thrill
of bathing in
the darkness,
bathing in his
cologne.
you loved the
moonlight that
barely peeked
into his truck
windows.
it made him a
mystery.
his lips, his love,
the orange mango
trident on his mouth
were a familiar that
you could never
get enough of.

you aren't perfect.
i'm not sure you
ever were.

you wanted to
make the same

mistakes all
teenage girls your
age were making.

you wanted to make
the mistake of
falling in love.
you wanted to make
the mistake of
fully living in
the present,
with no consideration
of your future.

i am envious of you.
these mistakes have
molded me into
a woman who takes
life too seriously.
i live life comfortably
on the edge,
never having the
desire to jump,
afraid of the sea
of possibilities.
i still dream but
my dreams are
comfortable for me.

you were never perfect.
  you embraced your
imperfections.
 you made them beautiful.

i wish i could do the same.

Before the Falling

it was his swag:
the confidence
that seeped
through his
pores like
sweat on one of
those humid
july days.
maybe it was his
smile:
the way he took
it everywhere
with him or the
way he used it
as if admiring
my existence.
whatever it was
about him,
not only did i
want him to
be mine,
i wanted
to be his.

Journey, Circa 2010

my hurts:
written in the
  sand dunes of
my soul left
 to be washed
away by tsunamis
  that sink your
greatest fears away.

my blessings:
  chiseled upon
a heart of stone and
  left to be found
by archaeologists.

my mistakes:
  written on the
leaves of my
  growing tree,
blown away by the
  winds of maturity.

my dreams:
  written on the
shooting stars of
my subconscious.
as i believe,
   they come true.

Change

it is happening all around us. the seasons are changing:
the leaves live vibrantly on the limbs of
trees and they love and grow through the summer and
spring.
then they depart from the limbs but they always return.
the moon is phasing: touching lands near and
far. serving the ability to be in many places
at one time. never late on its arrival.
some transitions may be difficult to grow
through but remember the beauty in the changes
around you and realize, your evolution can be
just as beautiful.

i was familiar
with men who
broke hearts.
whose egos
bled from the
fangs of their teeth,
digging deep
into her skin.
injecting her with
his poison
his poison
his

love. the only
love he knew
how to give:
hard love,
tough love,
never gentle. never
compassionate.
never aware.

this was the man
i expected to show
up on my radar.

disconnected.
but present.
someone who loved

himself and needed
me to love him that
much more.
a robot: out of touch
with his feelings.
out of touch with mine.
someone who knew
their role and
played it well.

i was familiar
with men who
weren't familiar
with themselves.

then you
came along.
you restructured
the entire blueprint.

In The Beginning

it's about the one
who you stay up
with when the moon
has reached its peak,
declaring secrets
into shadows of
the night.
whispering i like you,
carried by tempted
winds, spreading
gossip amongst the
stars.
the sun fell
in the background
as gracefully
as you did for him.

Guardian

you carry buried
treasure in the
cage that protects
your heart,
pearls of magic
in the eyes that
cry for a love
that never was.

you carry love stories
in a heart that
no longer generates
butterfly flutters.

you never needed
protecting.
you were always
the protector.
you protect seas
of generations
in the design
of your womb.

you find hope
in the possibility
that you can birth
a generation of love,
a love that you believed
the world needed.

a love that was lost,
could never be traced.

Battlefields

there was a war
happening
on the inside.
i couldn't recognize
my heart anymore.
it had been colored in
bruises with your
name on it.
you signed it.

destroying me
became your
masterpiece.

there was a
  disconnect
between my
  sisters and me.
we all knew the
  same version of
him but dealt with
  him differently.
there was one
  thing we had in
  common:
we loved him.

my sister carried
  daddy's secrets
under the same
  cavities of her
heart that she
  carried her own.
she had always
  been good at
keeping secrets.
i envied this
  about her.

my sister carried
  and believed in
his humanity.

she always
searched for
the human in him
and she always
found it.
she found this
confidence,
this hope that love
was lost in
there somewhere.

i carried parts
of daddy that
i never wanted to.
parts of him that
burned holes
through my
memory but never
fell through.
i carried parts
of him that
filled my
heart with joy
and anger all
in the same cargo.

we all knew the
same version of
him but carried
him differently.

On Facing Your Demons

there is no perfect time
to face your truths.
you can break mirrors and
the fragments of your truth will be
scattered on cold bathroom tile,
with your blood left in its reflection.
your truths can
leave you collapsing into
yourself. over and over again.

when you do face them,
you will finally be able to hear and
count your heartbeats.
you will learn the comforts
in a sigh of relief.

From A Boat in San Jose del Cabo

you are like the
calm i imagine
whales feel
in the middle
of the ocean.
the breath of
fresh air they
feel with
every subtle
jump.
the comfort
they feel
once their
bodies are
submerged
back in the
freedom of
the ocean.

your hands are stronger
than you think.
they have endured
the stretching of limbs
in order to become the
hands of a woman
who needed to
carry things.

they have carried
waterfalls of tears
cried into the
drowning darkness
of many nights,
evidence appearing
under swollen eyes
the next morning.

they have held and
kept secrets that
should be buried
deep in the fog and
dark waters of
forgotten bayous.

they have suffered
the emptiness
of a love lost,
the emptiness of

the grasp of a
lover escaping and
losing the ability
to grab hold of
them again.

they have carried
the weight
of your baggage.
they kept the
baggage from
falling and breaking.
it kept the
contents from
spilling all
over the place.

your hands are
stronger than
you think.
trust them with
your heart.
allow them to hold
it. to protect it.

The Author

it was never written
  in a beautiful cursive
font or in a soft
  vintage print like
the dabs of a
  typewriter.
 it was written in
  bold, capital letters.

when the story
  of my being was
spoken, it was
  narrated in your
        voice.

you were the
author of my life.
the way you
penned it was
the way it was
supposed to be.

Before the Rainfall

i was the girl who wanted
to be filled with
sunshine and clear skies.
i wanted to be the reason for
gut-clenching laughter and conversation
that made you resent sleep.
i wanted to be loved by
everyone even if i wasn't
loved by myself.

that seemed worth it.

Good Morning Beautiful

i said it until
she believed it.
every morning
when the sun lay
  its rays on
corners of
  her skin,
summoning her
to wake up.
sleep settled
  in the crease
of her eyes.

i reminded her
  when she anticipated
how she was going
  to show up in the world.
when she anticipated
  her presentation
from the shoes that
  produced sores on
the soles of her feet
  to the blouse
that people told
  her brought out
her complexion.

at the wake of
  every morning,

the fall of
every night
i looked back
at her in the mirror
and reminded her
that she was beautiful.
she was enough.

When Demons Run Loose

when someone projects negative
energy into your life,
it is never about you.
it is about the demons they
are battling: demons that run
loose and find spaces to
cause destruction. they point
a finger at you and fail to realize
there are three more
pointing back at them.
they spit words of fire and
fail to realize they're the ones
burned by them.

it is never about you. never.

Views from the Shore

everyone tried to
swim to the
very depths
of me. they were
like sharks
craving to figure
me out. what
made you
different
was you
enjoyed
admiring
my beauty
from the shore.

Author of Your Life

be the painter of your own canvas:
paint your life exactly how you dreamed it to be.
write the song of your life that you want to dance to.
orchestrate the symphony that motivates you to
push through. this specific life was given to
you and to no one else. this life was given to you
to fall but to get back up. this life was given to you
to cry puddles of tears and to fall into your reflection
in that puddle later. this life is yours. you are the
author. no one else. no one else. but you.

Mishandled

i handed my heart
over to him, entrusting
its safety to him.

he didn't take care of it.

he left it in dark places.
when he returned it,
no longer did i recognize it.
it was no longer mine.
it had been tampered
with, it had become
a foreign object,
even to me.

while i trusted him
with it, my heart
trusted me to protect it.

On The First Time
Saying I Love You

we would talk
 on the phone for
hours at a time.
 it became a hobby,
second nature,
 we did it so much.
the goal was to
 avoid silence but
it would fall
 into the cracks
of the 'i love you' that we
 wanted to say
but couldn't.

'i need you,'
that we knew
 needed to be said
but there was this
 rule that you never
say anything first.

i stumbled.
 i tripped into
the words
i love you,
 they fell into our
 conversation.
you hesitated.
 you said it back.

i'm still not sure
you meant it the
first time you
said it.
but it never
mattered.

the conversation
continued,
as if nothing
happened.
as if our lives
would not be
changed from
three words that
seemed so simple.

i wondered who i
would end up
being for you.

there will always be
that one time:
 that one time
we laughed on
the cusp of
 drowning in
 a sea of
lovesick phrases.
 that one time
we watched the
 moon rise
sitting on top of
 rainbows
discussing how
 small and
imperfect
we were in
correlation
 to the moon.
 that one time
our bodies sent
electric magnetic
waves to the other,
 attracting the
connection of
 our hands,
of our souls.
 oh, but,
my favorite time,
that one time,

we did the
unthinkable
and tumbled
head first
in love.

Containers

i remember the day i escaped.
i brought all of my preserved
sanity and good girl will and
all the mistakes that suffocated
in the cage you kept me in.
and i learned how to breathe
  on my own.

Igniting Fires

one of the most
frightening parts
about being in
love is allowing
an imperfect,
flawed being
the honor of
igniting a fire in you.
taking on the risk
of them giving up
on everything
grotesque yet
beautiful your love
has become. and not
having the decency
to extinguish the flames.

you're trying to
  find your way.

you have let your
  passions slip
through the spaces
  between your
fingers.
you're simply
existing. some say
that's enough.

you have tried to
  find yourself in
the lives of everyone
  else but you have
been unable to.
 there's no room
   for you.

now, here you are,
  alone in your lane
watching everyone
  around you pass you by.

you are constantly
  planning towards
your happiness.
  you compose
affirmations about

your feelings,
you wish to remain
in tune with them.

there is something about
this sadness and anger
that carries a sense
of urgency.
you don't ignore it.
this lesson seems so
small in your world
right now.

it's pivotal later.

it teaches you
to not ignore those
rough emotions.
to get on the
surfboard, ride out
the waves of them.

you do just that.
you spend countless
nights, drowning
in tears and broken
prayers.
it is necessary.

i admire you.

you're the reason
why i am okay
with these
uncomfortable
  emotions.

  you're the reason
 why i no longer
 try to fight them.

i just let them hold
  me captive.

you're the reason
  for that.

Scarred Celebration

he pointed to a scar that i
believed had long faded.
i was familiar with
that scar. just like
i was familiar with
the way his forehead
creased when he
wasn't sure of a thing
or the way he
lightly snickered
before a burst of
laughter took over.

he was concerned.

he wanted to know
their stories.
he wanted to know
when they were born.
if i noticed that
any of them
started to die.
he wanted to know
about the ones present
and the ones that
no longer occupied
space on my body.
he wanted to know
if i missed any of them.

he pointed to my scars,
asked me if i loved

any of them.
asked me which ones
i appreciated.

he pointed to the scars
that were self-
inflicted. he ran his
fingers over them
gently as if the
wound were
still open. his tears
fell upon them as
if he had witnessed
my skin being unsealed.

i told him about
the nights that i would
witness my skin running
away from a blade.
a game of cat and mouse.
i told him about the silent
tears that fell loud.

he asked me why.
i told him it made
me forget.

he pointed to the ones that
i believed had long faded.

the wound heals,
no matter how
deep the cut.
it's the scar that may
never go away.

You Were Always Enough

i needed love to
be enough to
protect me from
all of the storms
i could not shelter
myself from.
i needed love to be
enough to comfort
me from all things
i refused to face.
i needed love to be
enough to protect
me from myself.
when from the
beginning, the one
person who was
always enough
was the one i
always refused
to face.

Striking Resemblances

the more my heart
tried to steer away
from him, the more
i wanted to love him,
the more i wanted for
him to love me.
sometimes it seemed
impossible for him
to love me.

was it hard to love
me because every
time he looked
at me he saw
himself and every
mistake he could
never forgive
himself for.

maybe he saw himself
when he looked at me

and he hated it.

Empty Mornings

good morning
to empty spaces
where your body
used to settle.
empty hellos that
we uttered in passing
under the roof
of our home:
strangers in the
morning time.

good morning
to cold coffee
that remained on
the kitchen counter,
a gesture of
forgiveness
that one so
helplessly missed.

good afternoon
to days going
by with only
you on my mind.
the stubbornness
kept our egos warm.

good morning
to empty spaces
where your body

used to rest.
empty spaces
that i would roll
into and allow my
body to sink into the
form that used
to be you.

not having you is foreign:
i don't want to understand it.

we must honor our
marks from love:
the dimples that
form in the
corners of our mouths
from engaging
in too much laughter
with the ones
we love.

we must honor the
lines from growth:
the cinnamon swirls
that have found
comfort in our thighs
from too much reaching
to touch the stars.

the designer bags
that rest comfortably
under our eyes,
from tears we've
cried into a sea
of dusk, in
the depths of
lonely and cold
queen-sized beds.

or the way we carry

love in ways
no one else
has carried it.

beauty and strength,
will and dedication
have attached themselves
to us and they're not
letting go.

When the Silence is Deafening

i'm not sure which
i feel sorry
for the most:
the silence that
stumbled into
our conversation or
the words that sat
uncomfortably in the
passages of our throats,
wishing and waiting
for us to allow them to
escape; to breathe
the life back into us.

Lessons Never Learned

i would never know
how to love you,
that scared me.
you were the type
of person who
deserved to be loved.

i wasn't taught
how to love.

love was destructive
and complicated
and nothing i ever
wanted to give,
nothing i ever
wanted to receive.

how did you love
so well?
how did you know
which dark corners
to love and which ones
to stay away from?
how did you know
when to give love
unconditionally and
when to take a step
back and let me
figure out how to
love me?

you made the greatest
impossibilities possible.
you showed me how
to love despite not
knowing how.
you found my hand
in the dark.
you guided me.

who was going to
guide you?
who was going to
remind you every day
that you were lovable?
who was going to
convince you that
you were a dream
come true?

maybe you didn't
need to be guided.
maybe you knew how
to find the light
from the darkest of
moments.
maybe you didn't
need to be convinced.
maybe loving you the
only ways i knew how,
maybe loving you the
way you loved me,

maybe it was enough.
and maybe enough
was enough for you.

Soul Shields

she created a shield
around her soul:
they could have
her heart but
not her soul.
for her heart is
what concocted
the butterflies
that fluttered
when she thought
she was
falling in love.
and her soul
protected those
same butterflies if the
flutter ceased.

Asphyxiate

i need space:
i need to
find comfort
in my
circumference:
you're surrounding
that.

i need to reconnect
with me:
i am losing
her in you.

i have located
uncomfortable angles,
they are creating
a barrier
between my
love for you and
the love i have to
have for me.
no one ever
taught me how
to separate the two.

we pretended to be
blinded by
the complications
of mixing two
completely different
equations and

expecting
perfect answers.

it seems like the
moment my body and
my mind have synced
up, making a
mutual agreement
to leave,
the force within you
finds ways to keep me:
it's smothering.

On the Little Girl Who Hides Inside of Me

there is a little girl.
she stands with her
chin sinking into
her chest.

this little girl lives
within the oceans
of me and
she is sinking.

she never left.

she is wounded.
she still feels the
pain from the past.
she has blinded
herself to what
the future holds.
how beautiful it is.

she is wounded.
the little girl inside
of me is wounded.
broken into mosaics
arranged across
my spirit.
every time i try
to pick up one of
the pieces, i get cut.
she tells me

"not yet. i'm not
ready to heal."

Dirty Laundry

i have this load of
hate that is piled
on top of my heart.
i'm not sure what
to do with it.
i considered cleansing
it and purifying it
with love but the
stains are so tough
that would take
a lifetime.

the most delicate
form of nature.
the carrier of heartbreak
and generations.
never fix your
being to
falsely tamper with
the spirit of a
woman, becoming
the reason for her
downfall. for you shall
never endure the
pleasure of
basking in the
glory of her
breakthrough.

Filling Spaces with Silence

the silence was
suffocating.

i grew up
used to the
silence.

but i never wanted
to remember
how uncomfortable
it was with you.

there is something
you have to know
about me.
i learned there were
only three ways to
deal with your
problems:
you deal with
them with
destruction, then
you fill spaces
with silence
and then roars
that make the
ground shake.

i've never found
peace in the
destruction;

the roars were always
  deafening.
the silence, was always
an uncomfortable
space to occupy
and i never wanted
to get used to
 uncomfortable
   with you.

Ghost Trails

there are ghosts
they linger
through chambers
where she
pushed haunting
memories
that she wished
to forget.

she had problems
with letting go,
afraid of forgetting
the experiences
that molded her,
the heartbreaks
that allowed her to
appreciate a
mended heart.

the lies surrounding her
like bad karma
helped her find
comfort in the truth.

she knew she
would rather grow
from new experiences,
than break from
old ones.

i needed you to
love me in ways
i knew you couldn't.
i needed you to tell
me the mistakes i made
were okay to make:
i was human.
i needed you to not
make me feel like i
was the only one in
this life and the next to
ever create a spill
of mistakes and not
clean them up.

i needed you to hear me.
listen to me.

but, i was drowned
out by your voice.
your authority.

i was drowned out

by you.

Crossroads

no longer are we
connecting, simply
just being. we got
trapped in a web of
the norm of things,
abandoned all of
the sweet talk,
intimate gestures
that got us here in
the first place.
i no longer want
to be trapped.
i want to be free,
returning to the
people we both
fell in love with.

Identity

the mirror and i:
enemies,
engaged in
  constant
confrontation.

it never reflected
   the person
i wanted to be.
i fell victim to
assigning myself
different names and
   identities,
always too
  ashamed
      to be me.

i wanted to be
  any woman
but myself.

walking the streets
with a hijab on
became shameful.
i didn't care if you
thought god would
love me more.

people watched me,
  constantly.

my features weren't
strong enough to
be from a part of
the world they knew
nothing about.
my voice wasn't
laced with
an accent you had
to listen carefully
to understand.

but a black woman in
a hijab seemed
to be a threat,
nonetheless.

they could never get
my name right,
i convinced them that
it was something else,
that i was someone else.

it never felt real.
i never felt real.
i became wrapped up,
consumed in hiding
behind false identities.

when the real me
finally emerged
we were strangers

to each other,
strangers that had
been together their
whole lives.

For Everyone Who Has Loved Someone Who Couldn't Reciprocate

don't lose yourself so much in the love
you think you deserve that you
begin to settle for less.
if your spirit is already damaged,
don't allow anyone to
bruise and break and tear it more.
do not allow anyone to convince
you that you're just a star in their
universe; you are the universe.
your love deserves to be appreciated.
your flaws deserve to be
nurtured. and you,
you deserve the
highest and purest form of love.

Gentle Reminder

when you learn to love yourself
unconditionally and wholeheartedly,
you teach others how to love you
the same and you will never accept or
expect a love less than you deserve.

papa was a poet.

i was told that
when you house
the soul of a
creative,
you feel pain
differently than
other souls.

pain becomes
standing in
front of a train,
getting hit and
doing it all over
again.

pain becomes
watching love
walk in and out
of your life with
no idea how to
make it stay.

as a creative,
you are timeless.

you live with
happiness
differently.

when you feel it,
you try to hold
onto it
because with a
heart like yours,
it doesn't come
around often and
it never seems to
stay.

margaret.anna.marian.stephanie.
donna.vickie.melissa.

she carried elegance
like fine jewelry,
delicate pearls
strung on a
lifetime of wisdom,
impeccable diamonds
as exquisite as the
sparkle in her eyes.

she carried eloquence
like autumn leaves
adding a splash of
lovely to wind
blown trees.
the breeze drifted
to the smooth stride
in her step.
trees swayed in
her direction.

i always wondered
how she sat a top
her imperfections
but still resembled
a queen.

i stopped wondering
and became her.

because, it's never easy to love yourself

one day, i will love myself void of conditions. i will be present in the world proud of the woman i have become and am becoming. one day, i will fully trust my judgment and never second guess my decisions. i will give myself permission to walk away from all situations and people who do not serve an uplifting purpose in this life i have worked so hard to form. one day, i will sleep peacefully knowing that i am and always have been the only version of myself that i knew how to be.

i am a work in progress. we all are. one day, i will realize despite my mistakes and shortcomings, one thing i have always been is a masterpiece in the making.

Matters of the Heart

mind the gap:
the gap between
what my heart feels
is real and what my
mind tries to
protect me from.

my heart:
she was fed
this craving to
love long ago;
she's hopeless.

she takes up most
of that space
that is meant to
protect me and
fills it with love:
she sees the good
in everybody.

empty canvas

sometimes we are drawn into confused and lonely spaces. vulnerable spaces. spaces that lack confidence. spaces full of self-doubt. our canvases stand in silence, unpainted as we figure out our way through these spaces. there are times when this journey has to be our own but there is nothing like that reminder that strength is still holding onto you. that you're still beautiful even through the confusion. sometimes the rough emotions construct a hazy picture but the going through and the getting through the storm are what makes them so beautiful. so worth it.

Being You, Anyway

people tell you that you've changed
when you have broken out of the
minimal expectations they have
assigned to you and
discovered limitless possibilities.

be different, anyway.
be you, anyway.

My Favorite Book

i have memorized
the syllables
that grace pages
describing the essence
of your impeccable being.
highlighting parts of
you that deserve to be
explored more.
that deserve my
full attention.
i loved walking
my fingers
along your spine:
the thing that
kept you together.
the bridge that
brought us together.
the strength that
contributed to
the wholeness of you.
you were the metaphor
that had something to do
with gravity and us
and pushing love
into the plot.
i'll keep reading
you, adding chapters
to your life:
both of us the writer
and the muse.

Universal Reminders

who told her she
wasn't magic?
who told her
she wasn't a
cluster of
handpicked stars
from the universe?
who told her she
wasn't destructive and
hard to deal with?
who told her she
wasn't beautiful?
or phenomenal?
or enough?

who told her she
wasn't enough?

who forgot to tell
her that she was
the blueprint of
everything that exists,
has existed, and
will exist.
who forgot to remind
her of her
greatness?

she did.
he did.
they did.

you did.

i did.

From a Hotel in London

blessed even
when i feel
i've been cursed
by the outrages
of life.

loved and
loving even
when trapped in
a state of
vulnerability.

forever humbled
to be able to
witness and live
life void of
restrictions and
through the eyes
of none but
self.

everyone
else's vision has
already been
captured.

Blessed Rising

take notes from the sun: there is beauty in rising
slowly. brew a cup of fresh new starts
filtering out the worries, fears and doubts
of yesterday. sip slowly: indulge yourself by
finding new ways to make your day
beautiful. inspiring.
worth it.

Black Magic

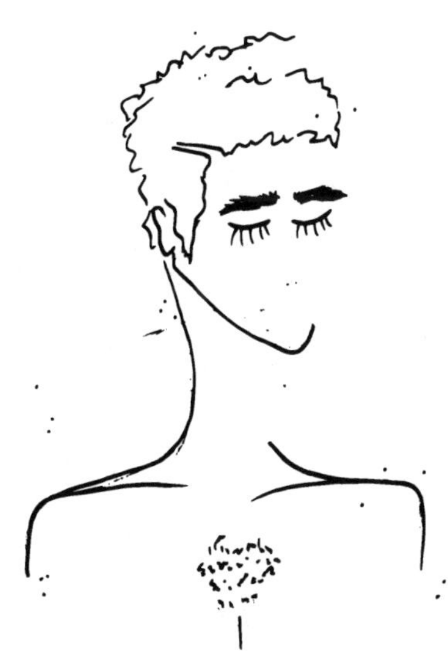

i celebrate you
like every day is
your birthday;
blowing out
candles when the
world sleeps,
filling our bellies
with laughter as
we hold our own
ceremony: dancing
through smokes of
incense and praising
the supreme that you
made it another day.

i honor you as if you
were adorned in
badges of victory:
your every failure
and success,
battle wounds infected
with stories to tell.

black men, i forgive you:
you have been fed
stories of make believe.
you never wanted to
be the reason for empty
spaces at dinner tables
or empty spaces mothers
are left to fill when your
absence was questioned.

you were made to
believe there was no

way you could be a father
with flaws so you chose
not to be a father at all.

black men, i appreciate you.
  those of you who rise
up in the face of a world
  who sees you as a threat.
a world that wants to
  get rid of you:
ban your very existence.

i have heard once before:
black men are kings
with no kingdom.

you are ascendants
of greatness. derivatives
of palaces in Africa;
adorned in royal garb and
drinking from fountains
that you could see
the world through.

black men,
i celebrate you.

though this place
is not your home,
allow the world to
bear witness from
the pits of your
throne as you
rebuild and reign;
  continue to reign.

A Love That Was Ours

i love that you're with
me no matter what.
if i'm about to ride a wave,
you're throwing on your
swim gear prepared for any
tsunami that tries to stop us.

when i feel defeated,
you pick up the boxing
gloves willing to
fight my battles.

i love that you're with me
no matter what.

despite the forces that have
tried to bring us apart,
you always told me,
"i'm with you because
i want to be."
none of it mattered.

our love was not the drama,
the defeats we fought through,
the doubts that contaminated our
surroundings.

our love was our love.

Because, I Have to Let Go

i love you but i can no longer give you permission to show up in my life anyway you like. i can no longer give you permission to treat me like a stranger until you need me. i am not setting these bounds to be rude or to break you. i'm setting them because it's the only way i have learned to love myself and to put me back together again. i'm doing this because if you're not going to respect me, i need to respect me enough to know what's right or wrong; enough or not enough in my life. what's healthy or unhealthy. what is toxic or nurturing.

Prison Letters

From:
To: Daddy

Day 1

~~dear dad~~

i never called you dad.

~~dear papa~~

it was what we called you growing up.
i haven't spoken to you in months.

there were words that
rained in my
head and i
waited for them
to create a
storm on the page.

how are you?

an unfit question to ask, considering
the circumstances.

Day 63

your birthday landed a couple of months after they took you. i wondered how you'd celebrate. my heart broke. even though every part of me that i tried to ignore told me even if you were here, i wouldn't have seen you on your birthday. possibly wouldn't have even called. my heart still...

broke.

i bought you a journal. you were a writer. you were who i owed gratitude for this gift. you. i couldn't imagine being locked away. behind bars. like a caged bird. so i sent you a journal. someone told me i should sign the inside. i didn't know what to say. "i hope you're well." i misspelled well and had to cross it out and rewrite it. i wrote in pen. i wrote that i loved you and signed my name. the journal was no longer perfect. i ruined it...

i seemed to ruin
a lot of things.

Day 88

i would ask about you. every week. i would ask in whispers; ashamed that no one would understand my concern. but, no one every judged my concern. they told me how you were and sometimes told me you asked about me. it made me feel good but it felt crazy all in the same breath. we both asked about each other but didn't speak to each other. the irony.

she said you
wanted to see me.

my heart raced.

she said you
wanted to see me.

i didn't know what
that would look like.

she said you
wanted to see me.

but there were
conditions.
i could only see
you understand
certain circumstances,
rules provided by you.

i became angry. you hadn't changed. nothing had changed. even considering the circumstances… under any circum stances… under all circumstances, you had to be in control. you always had to be in control. i refused to give into that control.

i always gave into that control.
                    into your ego.
i fed it.
i satisfied its
  cravings.
 i was done.
 it was time for
   your ego to starve.

Day 95

i considered giving into your commands… your demands. i just wanted to see you.

Day 125

i asked questions:

what does his hair look like? has it grown? does he have much facial hair? what does he wear? do they really wear those orange jumpsuits? do you talk to him behind a glass? what does he do all day? does he have to work? what's he reading? has he written much? what's he writing about? what's he thinking about?

does he tell you?
does he tell you?
does he tell you?

Day 147

"the secret of life, though, is to fall seven times and to get up eight times."
- paulo cohelo

how many times had you fallen and got back up? i heard it was never easy to get up after a fall. after falling so many times. i heard it wasn't easy. could you consider this a fall? when would you get up… when will you rise?

Day ...

i stopped counting the days you were gone. i stopped asking how you were; which had really become me asking if you had asked about me. i stopped asking. i stopped wondering if you wanted to see me and if you'd one day summon for me.

i stopped needing you.

Day ...

"one is loved because one is loved. no reason is needed for loving."
- paulo cohelo

they said you were getting out soon. they had been saying that. but there was a certainty in their voices. the language was different this time. it was foreign because it felt like it was actually going to happen.

Day ...

they said you were getting out today. my heart raced and my breathing increased. i fell to the floor and cried... you called me and told me you wanted to see me.

in the middle of a panic attack.

i said okay. and i came. i arrived. i showed up

because i needed you.

and i didn't want to.

Home

papa came home.
grandma's house
was filled with
laughter and the smell
of spaghetti cooking
on the stove and
garlic toast in
the oven and an
authentic and genuine
and beautiful aura
fed us.

papa came home.
his laughter was
within arm's
length. i could
feel its warmth.
i could touch it.
it fed me.

my little sister
played with the
other children but
would snap back
to a reality she
had never wanted
to get used to.
she would run
back up the

stairs and make sure
he was still there.

she would hold his
face in her
small palms.
run her fingers
through his hair.
she would kiss
his cheek.
and return to
playing hide and seek.

his presence fed her.

Water For the Gardens in Your Soul

the moment i stopped worrying about how
everyone else was living their lives and
how others wanted me to live mine
was the defining moment that i began to
see my life through a
clearer lens and living this life
became a completely different experience.

On Holding Broken Pieces

you handled my
 brokenness better
than i did.
 you held it,
softly in calloused
 hands as if you
were afraid to
drop it and
 break it even
more.
 as if you were
afraid that
 your rough hands
would damage it
 more than it
 already was.
you cradled my
 loneliness better
than i did.
 you held it,
closely. you comforted
 it, reminded it
that it was not alone
 after all.

Admit It

we can all be good at pretending:
that “nothing is wrong”
that “i’m okay”
that “i don’t need anything.”
admit when everything is wrong.
be comfortable with saying
you’re not okay. if you need some
extra love, a little more attention,
a hug, say that. it’s okay to say that.

too often we attach
our heartbreaks and the
people who caused them to love.

love is not the broken heart.
love is new beginnings. god's smile.
pillow talk. fresh laughter.
butterflies dancing the merengue
on the edge of your soul.

love is witnessing sun rays
reach through the clouds and
grab hold of mountaintops. the
sigh from being in awe of
cotton candy sunrises.
love is a dream fulfilled. dancing
barefoot in the rain.

love is the breath you
try to catch every time
you see the one who makes
your heart soar enter the room.

love is the poem with all
the right words never written.
never thought of.

conversations you don't have at the dinner table

i placed blame on
you like the
place settings at
the dinner table:
fork, big fork to
the left, salad
fork next to that.
put ego across
from self, they
enjoy talking
to each other.

i placed you on
the wrong side
never the right
and i put nothing
beside you.

i was convinced
that you'd do
something,
that you'd do
anything to
break
me.

but let's talk about:

who broke you?

who was the first
  store clerk to
follow you around
the grocery store
when you were
sent to buy
your mother milk
and eggs to
make apple
cinnamon muffins that
made the whole house
  smell like
fall leaves.

who was the first store
clerk to follow
you around because,
well, you looked like
the guy who almost
robbed them last
week only you were
a little bit taller and
your hair was cut
shorter. and you
  didn't dress like
      he did, no you
were dressed a
  bit more sophisticated

  but you still
looked the part.

who was the first
person to convince
you that the only
significant role
you'd play was
  a thug.
 was it the cop
who always pulled
you over because
from the outside
your thunderbird looked
like it'd be carrying
something illegal
  on the inside.
and that wasn't just
  one time,
it was every time
you passed him by.

who was the first
  person to not
                        believe in you
                        to accuse you
                        to abuse you
                        to bruise you
                        to take you
                                        for granted
                        to tell you they
                                        couldn't love you
                                        wouldn't love you.

who told you that
you weren't lovable.

who broke you.
who broke you.

i need to know.

we need to have
these lost

conversations.

Type A

i'm not sure what
type of woman i
was supposed to
be for you.
did i need to be strong?
because sometimes i can't
carry my own weight.
did i need to be
lovable?
i can be. sometimes
i'm not.
sometimes my feelings
get hurt.
i cry when i see other
people cry.
i get angry for no reason.
often times,
i can smile through the rain.
i can laugh when it hurts.
and i can love you.
i can love you.
is that enough?

On Standing in Love

i fell in love not realizing that
i didn't have to. not realizing that i
could fully be in love.
i could stand straight in love.
be every piece of myself.
that no falling was necessary.
and if at any point i did fall,
you would be my safety net.
you would catch the fall and
embrace it. you would cushion it.
you would take my hand
and show me what it looks like
to stand in my own again.

The Wrong Hero

are we setting our
expectations too high
when we require
love to be the hero?
to save us from all
things we feel we
cannot save ourselves from.

would you expect for
love to be the hero
if you were trapped
in a burning building.
your judgment so clouded,
you couldn't see pass
the smoke at the exit sign
right in front of you.

what if love didn't
save you and you had
to save yourself?
would you rejoice in
the powerful ability of self?
the ability that you
believed you lacked?
or would you fully ignore
your own superhero
capabilities and be upset
and disappointed that
love wasn't enough
to save you.

what is so wrong
with you being enough?
are we expecting too
much when we require
love to solve the
problems that we
give up on?
the problems that we
should not even want
another spirit to
solve for us. the ones
that become too much
to carry, the load
becomes too heavy that
we become open,
selfish rather, to throw
that weight on love.

or when we expect
love to be our one
and only security?
the only thing that
we expect to protect
us from all that we're
afraid to protect
ourselves from.

because what happens
when we believe
love has failed?
when the imperfections
of the individual we

have attached love to
begins to reveal itself?
do you give up?
or do you become all
things for love that
you once needed
love to be for you.

it was not until
this point that
you realized all
things that transpired
before now were
setting you up for
the beauty of the
moments within this
new year.

you never knew
what to expect but
you went into this
year differently
than the others.

you approached this
year claiming what was
already yours.

you claimed your
future and everything
in it that you wanted
and you received it.

you're the reason
i knew it was
all worth it.
something like
the double rainbow
after a storm.

a butterfly out of
a basic brown cocoon.
the victory after
many triumphs.
it was not until then
that i realized all things
good and bad were
worth it.

i wouldn't call this
year a rebirth.
it is more like a
discovery of the
woman you had
been all along.
there is a sudden
calmness and appreciation
that has come over you.

and i love that.
i cherish that.
i appreciate that.

start with the soil.
you cannot plant your
seeds just anywhere.
find soil that you
know can withstand
all things that may
attempt to tamper
with or break down
your foundation.

after securing the soil,
select the seeds you
wish to plant.
plant the seeds that
you know will
  be nurturing and grow
into beauty but whose
beauty could also make
other things grow.
plant seeds of trust,
communication,
friendship. allow
  them to grow.

there will be
  bad days.
don't fret if
  all that you
have planted in
  your garden
begins to wither;

they just need more
attention.

as long as you
continue to grow in love,
you will blossom forever.

Love Note 001

your smile is a refreshing
presence after a chaotic day.
you were the calm before,
after and in the midst of the storm.

Humble Abode

you are home,
the one who provides
shelter to my heart.

your words,
my soul's food.

your arms, the only
comfort i need
when faced with
life's collisions.

your kiss, my sanctuary.
it is within the
delicacy of your lips
that i seek refuge.

you are a representation
of new beginnings.
you represent the broom
that dusted the cobwebs
that clouded my vision.

you represent love in
every aspect of the word:
all that is beautiful and
right about us.

A Flower in Her Own Right

i have always loved watching flowers
bloom and have always wished that the
budding and blossoming and
wilting and re-budding of my own
journey could be just as beautiful.

Love Language

accepting and understanding someone else's love
language is complicated. we have a certain way that
we want to be loved. when someone comes along
with their own ways of speaking and showing
love, we reject it. people love the only way
they know how, just like you. love is about
learning and growing. some translations of love
have been hard to understand but
i'm learning to and i'm learning that as long
as the love language comes from
a space of pure love, it can't be wrong.

Building Together or Not at All

i can't sacrifice my dreams
  for anyone else.
that's asking me to
  sacrifice my happiness for yours;
i worked hard for that.
i can help you build
  but i can't destroy or
neglect the architecture of
  my dreams to focus on yours.

The Things You Became

you were the poem
i repeated to
myself in mirrors
when the world slept.

you were the secret
that i whispered to
the moon and the stars;
they blushed when
i spoke of you.

you were the prayer
i chanted into empty
palms and the amen
i declared at the end.

you were the
exhale at the end
of deep breaths.

you were the wind
beneath my
wings: you showed
me how to soar,
proved to me that i
had the potential to fly.

Holding On When You Need to Let Go

i remember how
inevitable it
felt to let you go.
how it felt like
carrying fire and
always getting burned.
i grasped this idea
that you could change.
the thought alone
calloused my idea of hope.

Love Note 002

you became the love notes
that were never written.
you carry memories that
have runneth over from my
heart to yours. giving our
memories double the space
to be celebrated. when our
hearts have reached capacity,
we carry remaining memories
on the ledge of the
windows to our souls.
for when people look into them,
all they would ever see is love.

there are risks in being voiceless.
there are risks that lie in not learning,
honoring or allowing the gift of
expressing yourself.

this is remaining closed in the bud.

there are risks in blooming.
in expressing yourself.
in loving yourself.
that risk lies in the hearts of others.
sometimes people cannot handle that.
they cannot handle the power of
one having their own voice.
they cannot handle the power of one
knowing and fully loving themselves.
there is so much beauty in loving and
knowing and honoring self.

although the blooming may
not be freedom for them.
it is freedom for you.

today and every day be open
to loving yourself.
be open to the power of
expressing yourself. be open to
honoring yourself.

On Getting to Know You Over and Over Again

i want to always get to
know you. i want to
become reacquainted with
your likes and dislikes.
your dreams and all that
keeps you up at night. i
want my heart strings tugged
every time you discover a new
flaw and it happen to be
the one that i believed
made you perfect.

On Finding Someone to Nurture Your Brokenness

it's inevitable: we have all
experienced brokenness.
we have experienced the uncomfortable
ways it has attached itself to
our bodies. we have experienced
the shattering pieces
ruining us and bruising us.
these shattered pieces
that will not allow us to forget
that there is something damaged
about us.

one day, you will find someone who
will selflessly help you pick up
those broken pieces and
reconstruct yourself.
you will find someone who
values the flawed
human you are; they'll find
beauty in that. they'll find
love in that. and in that, they'll
find truth.

Love Note 003

be with someone who you
are comfortable sharing
silence with. someone who
doesn't always have to fill the
silence with noise, someone who
is comfortable with the space
silence takes up but doesn't fill.

be with someone who is okay
with you downloading your
thoughts and long days and
rough patches and energy into
them. someone who doesn't
take it as their own but will
help you carry the load
while you sort through it all.

be with someone who, no matter
what you're going through,
you can see them through the
storm, holding an umbrella.
still ready and willing to protect
you even though you've
had to adapt to climates that
were sometimes unpleasant
to grow through.

Not so Super, Woman

i used to have super powers:
i used to be able to shape shift in the
presence of those who could never
accept me for who i truly was.

i used to be able to
transform into
the woman
anyone needed me
to be.
the woman that
they expected me
to be.

How You Know You've Found Love

when you have someone who holds on when
your demons are pushing and kicking
them away; you've found love.

when you have someone who can
gaze past the lies that you tell:
"i'm okay," "it's nothing," and pulls out truths
that you have never wanted to face;
you've found love.

when you have someone who keeps
you and your truths warm as you become
accustomed to them;
you've found love.

when you have someone who expresses
the beauty in you and the beauty in
mountains and oceans and other worlds,
all in the same breath,
you've found love.

when you have someone whose
smile gives you the same
feeling as witnessing god painting
the skies baby pinks and pick me up yellows,
you've found love.

Seeds for the Gardens in Your Soul

there are some people who cannot stand
to see you win. there are some people who
cringe at the thought of your happiness.
then, there are people like you.
people who rise above the doubt.
who realize their art is greater than any hate.

it's people like you who change worlds.
who restructure universes.

A Different Kind of Home

i never thought my heart nor my hands
nor my soul was of capacity to
hold all of your heart:
it has always been too big.

i promised myself many moons ago that
i would only allow space to carry
my own insecurities and my own love and
that space was only for me.

then you came along.

your willingness to find space
for me and all of the heartbreaks
i carried and my baggage of doubts
and my love,
proved to me that our hearts,
our hands and our souls
are built for this.
they are made for this.

i learned to find space for
you and let you in and its
felt like home ever since.

Love Note 004

if i would have known romantic and
pure and intimate and forever love
looked like you and felt like this,
i would have found you lifetimes ago.

Love Affairs with the Sun

the sun loves kissing
your skin. she summons
for the wind to whisper
her sweetest desires
through your hair.
her favorite part is
reaching out through
feathers in the clouds,
planting her sunrays on
bare parts of your skin,
deeper than a lover
ever could.
the sun sneaks through
bedroom blinds,
planting soft kisses
to assist with your
morning rise.
you don't even
realize how it has marked
you until your lover
compliments you
on the foreign
sweetness in your skin.

Cheers to New Chapters + Baggage Left Behind

i left the baggage
  at the door
not because i
  didn't want it
anymore
  it just became
too much to carry.
  i blew the dust off,
finally finding
  the courage to
start a new chapter,
  the strength to
rebuild my queendom
  between streams of
unparalleled cracks
  of insecurities.
i am a witness:
  god can make detached
branches fruitful again.

Holding Love Towards the Clouds

i wondered how high i
could hold you.
you deserved to be placed on a
pedestal that touched the clouds.

i wondered how long
i could carry you with me:
forever never seemed long enough.
eternity was fast approaching.

i wondered how much i could love you.
every day it seemed to become impossible,
too good to be true: i knew i loved you
more than i did yesterday and couldn't
imagine loving you even more tomorrow.

truth be told, i always did.

Autumn

she was the color of fall:
warm and vibrant.
her hair sacred silk from
ancient times.
her golden skin looked as if
it had been dipped in the
excess of the sun rays:
she was beauty herself.

Thoughts from Allenspark

your demeanor represented
the calmness of the mountains.
your love set me in motion
like secret waterfalls hidden
behind snowcapped hills
that protected them from
everything not as pure
and magical.
you wrapped your love
around me like clouds
embrace mountaintops.
sometimes, you let go in order
for me to know what journeying
and loving was like without you.
other times you just held me,
as we watched the beauty of
our world unfold.

Black Girl Magic

black women, i
celebrate us.
the crowns that
sit upon our heads
are invisible to
the world.

rays of sunshine
peeked beneath
your skin.
you are shimmers
of gold.
a confetti of colors.
you are hues of
caramel swirls.
midnight sky.
rich mocha.
mi prima calls
her hue cafe con leche.

you are "girl sit up
straight. don't fall into
your spine." and
"you better not get
that hair wet," as if
it were a sin. you are
"girl, sit with your
legs close.
protect your
universe."

the words that fall
out of your mouth:

chants. you carry
the majestic ability
to hypnotize with
the golden silk laced
in your diction.
with the hallelujahs
laced in your language.

girl, you are a
praise song. they treat
you like a myth. an urban
legend. even if they
touch you, they'd never
know you were real.
is it real?
is she real?
can i touch it?
as if running their fingers
through your black girl
magic would prove you
to be real.

you are a hymn.
a hum to the moonlight.
you carry the
ability to have
conversations with god.
you have always
been magic. it's not
your fault no
one ever noticed it.

because, loving you

because, loving you
influenced me to look
forward to the poems
i would write about
you later.

i traced the rhythm
in the curves of your lips
with my eyes as you spoke.

i analyzed the way
your hands danced as
you became the narrator
of your day.
i closed my eyes quickly
and listened slowly
as your voice awakened
parts of me that the sun
could never kiss: heart and soul.

because, loving you
made me realize:
you were the poem
i had never written.
you were the poem that
was new and beautiful and
exhilarating and life
changing and perfect.
you were perfect.
there was no way
i could write
anything so perfect.

Sunshine for the Gardens in Your Soul

there is a fixation surrounding this idea that you cannot love someone until you love yourself. it was not until i knew and realized that i was capable of fully loving someone else that i realized the possibility that i could love myself the same, if not greater. i was so in love that i told myself that i wanted to love me just like that: selflessly and freely and purely. not everyone is going to love the same. not everyone is going to fall in love with themselves the same. it's all a part of the ride.

A War on Daughters

your daughter is
a war zone.
her mind a weapon
of mass destruction.
a mind you filled
with memories and
things and words
that destroyed her.

your daughter is
a war zone.
she stands on the
front line hoping
that the sacrifice
would spark
a change.
no one ever told
her that those on
the front line
always go first.

your daughter is
a war zone.
she is familiar
with every scar
on her body.

she knows that
this scar is from

your belt,
when she cradled
herself in the corner
of her bedroom
begging you to stop.
begging anyone
to make it stop.

she knows that
the scar on her soul
is when you called
her out of her name,
the word pierced
straight through,
causing a fire
inside of her.
that scar is
what's left.

she knows that
the scar on her
heart is from you
loving her all the
ways you knew how

but it never being enough.

**Nights of Mingling
With the Moon**

honoring my womaness.
honoring the ability and
the beauties in being flawed.
honoring the spirit of
love that remains pure;
the spirit that i have often
times tried to tamper with.
never realizing love cannot
  be tampered with.
honoring my otherness.
my ability to be different
than all with no desire
  to shape shift.
honoring the divinity
  in my blackness.
honoring love tonight.
honoring me tonight.

Your Country

you were cut from a
different fabric
distressed edges,
centers of fine silk.

you were cut from
women who
grew love and
happiness and
families from
seeds of nothing.
women who were
magical, who
created life from
stolen dreams.

you were cut
from goddesses.
mothers of
generations.
royalty flows
like rivers
through your
bloodlines.

you were cut
from women
who carry love
like they carry

children, first in
their womb where they
grow and where
butterflies rest
then forever:
in their heart.

you were cut from
women who kept their
lonely company,
women who made
the broken parts of
them their companions.

you were cut from women
betrayed by love,
women who loved
anyway.

these are the
women you
were raised by.
the women you
blossomed from.

prose

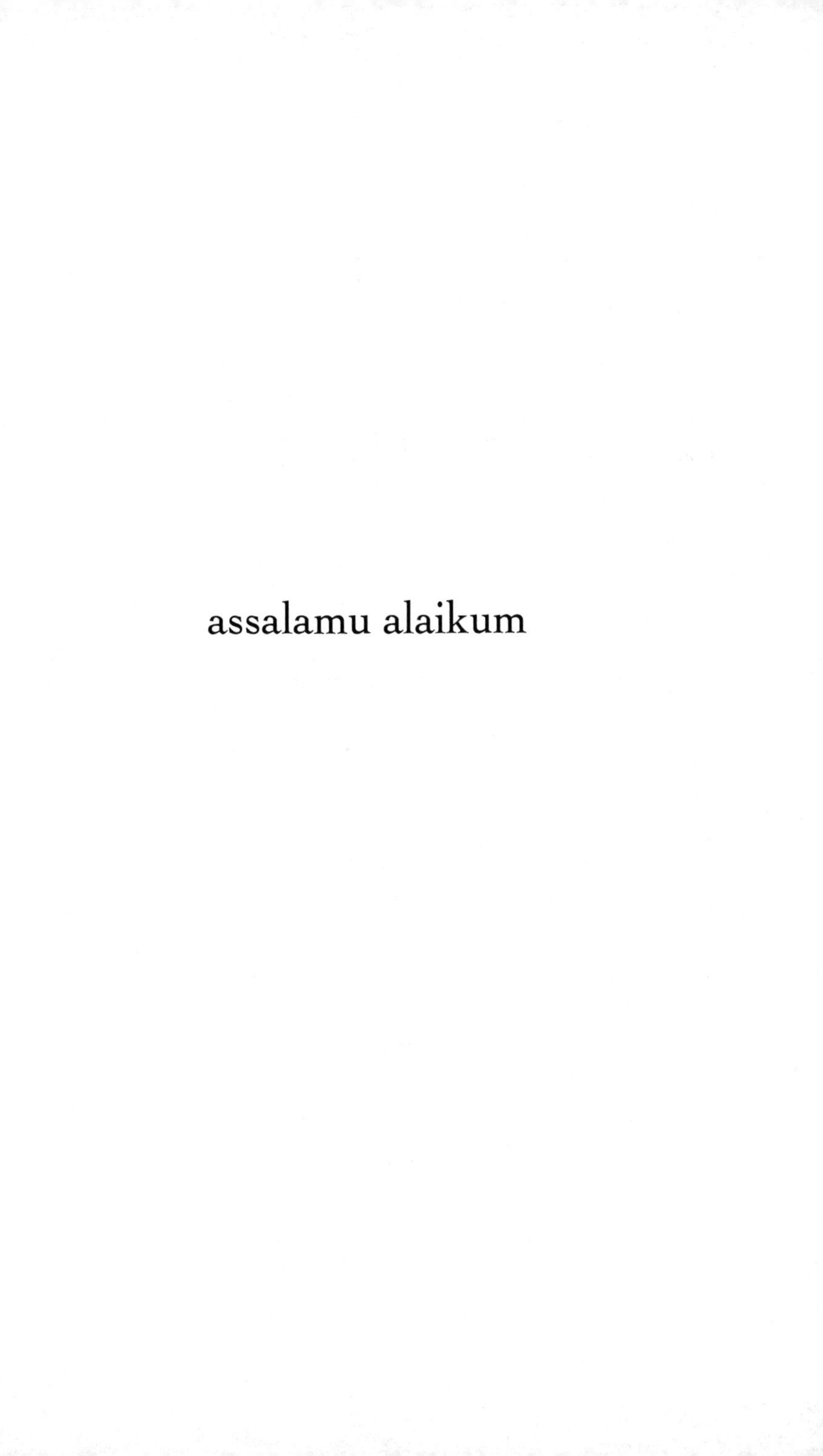

assalamu alaikum

one.

her and god never had a formal introduction.

she couldn't remember who the first person was to tell her about god. possibly her grandma who believed in his power. believed that the possibility of all things came from him.

she could've learned about him from her father. he believed that you lived life to please god. that god saw everything. saw you sin. he believed god punished us when he couldn't. god had his back.

by the time she was seven years old, she was afraid of him.

by the time she was seven, she was living her life to please two people: her father and god.

they seemed like the same person.

she never thought she would ever get to know him. he seemed

untouchable. unlovable. unavailable.

two.

they adopted islam as their religion: everybody was something and this is what they were. there wasn't any special conversion ceremony. they were told and they were.

she was very familiar with what they were not. the only other religion she was familiar with was christianity. her father labeled it the white man's religion. so, she wasn't surprised when he found something else for them to be.

she had a problem with labels.

she felt like labels carried so much weight. labels presented you as something or someone other than yourself. labels confused her; she wasn't sure who she was outside of them.

every friday, when they went to the mosque, she questioned (in her head) why women had to sit in the back and the men in the front. she had a problem with that.

she questioned why the women rarely looked the men in their eyes when they spoke to them. she had a problem with that.

she knew she never looked daddy in his eyes because she was afraid of him. was it the same thing?

she wondered if prayers were still valid if a woman lead them.

she figured it was this label: islam. this label: muslim. she figured it was the label that made men feel greater than and better than the women.

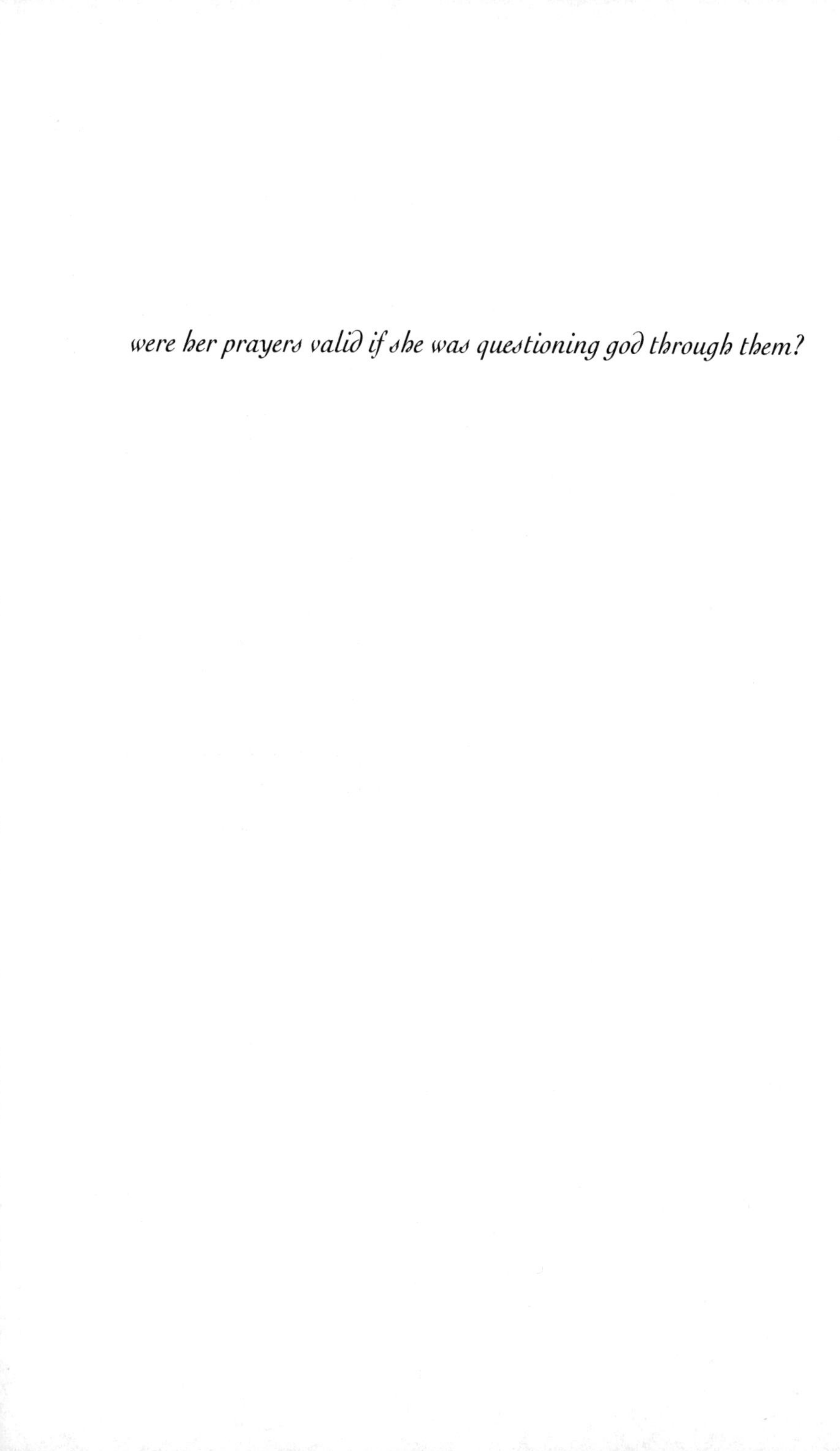

were her prayers valid if she was questioning god through them?

three.

she was twelve years old when she transitioned to womanhood.

tears shed as her womb shed. she didn't feel pain just fear.

her friends at school told her that when her period arrived, she'd be a woman. they associated being a woman with the older boys liking her because her breasts would be fuller. they associated being a woman with being able to kiss a boy. being able to have sex. being able to have a baby.

they told her all of that was bad. that she should refrain from all of it.

she went to an islamic school and dreaded going back when her period arrived.

there were rules. too many rules:

no singing.
no dancing.
no music.
always cover your head.
wear long sleeves.
cover your neck.

she was told that when you were on your period, you weren't allowed to pray, or touch the quran or speak any arabic.

"you have to wash. be clean. you're not clean," a teacher told her.

there were times she would still pray. she hated the way people looked at her when she sat in the corner of the prayer room watching as they prayed.

boys would break their prayer and look over at her; no smiles or smirks, they would just look.

she was the first girl in her sixth grade class to get her cycle.

the girls wouldn't make eye contact with her. they knew a secret that she didn't want them to know. everyone did.

they looked at her as if she were dirty. broken. tainted. from this thing that god gave her body the ability to do.

four.

every mistake she made reverted back to how much she disappointed god.

she felt he hated her and she hadn't become too fond of him.

the way he had been set up in her mind was that of a
jealous god.
an angry god.
a selfish god.

a god who wrote out her life to be claustrophobic to any mistakes. a story that she re-wrote full of them and she was being punished for it.

five.

there is a day. a day when the sun tucked itself in the pockets of clouds.

she was in trouble. she returned home too late or was talking on the phone too long or didn't hear him calling her name and answered after the second time; the reason for the punishment never mattered.

he always found a reason.

this time was different.

her father was calm. not destructive like he usually was.

everything stayed in place. there were no scars that she would remember later that dishonored her body. everything stayed in place.

her father insisted that there was no need for punishment this time. he insisted that god was taking her beauty away and that punishment was greater than anything he could ever do.

was it god who was now bruising her? re-arranging things out of place?

she observed herself in the mirror more than she had ever done. she tried to find what had been different.

she convinced herself that her father was right: the bags under her eyes seemed to hang lower. the pimples on her face never seemed to go away. she noticed her left eye was significantly lazier than the right. she tried to look into her heart; to see if god had bruised that as well.

she didn't like god because he seemed to love her father so much.

six.

she searched for god. she felt a need for his presence as she became older.

other methods to cope and deal with life's trials never seemed to work: the positive energy she released, disappeared. ignoring her issues brought them even closer to the surface.

her search began outside of the religion she grew up in. she wasn't pleased with the god who was presented to her; she believed she needed to find another one.

she searched for him in church and couldn't find him. she returned to islam and tried to re-establish a different relationship; a relationship on her terms. she couldn't find him there either.

she looked for god through storm clouds; tried to make him out. she talked to him and comforted him wanting to know the reason for the tears of rain and the anger that rumbled through the sky. she looked for him. she searched for him like a pair of keys. she could never find him.

seven.

it seemed like it took her a long time to find god.

but, then, she realized some people never do.

she rearranged this notion that you could only find god if you assigned yourself to a religion.

she found god in love.
she found god in the breaths she took.
she found god in the creations around her.
and in the creations within her:
the memories she created.
the love she created.
the happiness she created.

she found god inside of herself.

and she knew, keeping her so close, she could never lose her again.

for anyone who has ever lost someone

it was warm for december.

we weren't prepared for warm weather. sort of as unprepared as we were for his death. he had been sick for months. it was sudden. he wasn't feeling well; his energy was low. he went to the doctor. and they told him he was dying.

she said we had to pray for him. that we had to pray for him to recover. i did. i tried. but, i didn't know exactly what i was praying for. can you pray for someone who's already dying? do you pray for a miracle? or do you pray that when they do have to transition, that it's smooth, that it's painless. that when they do transition, there's someone who loves them on the other side to welcome them.

but i didn't pray for that. i didn't pray at all. i begged. i begged god not to take him. i begged god to heal him and to keep him on this earth with us. because we loved him and we needed him. and loving and needing him seemed like it was enough for god to keep him here.

it was warm for december.

the sun was hidden behind grey clouds and she peeked from behind every once in a while. there was a warmth that kissed the air.

it was warm for december.

we sat in rows. tears flowing down our cheeks. tears filled with the thought of memories that we wished to hold onto forever because that was all we had.

it was warm for december.

the sun finally found her way out of the clouds. she fell into the church through the colorful mosaic windows and touched us with her light as best she could. she knew we needed it.

because, although it was warm for december, our hearts were cold and filled with hurt and longing. our hearts fought to escape our body. the broken pieces tore and damaged our spirits. the weight of the longing and the hurt and the emptiness became too much for our bodies to carry.

too much for our hearts to carry.

we just needed a few more words with him. one more dance with him. one more laugh with him. we needed to take one more step with him. utter the words, "i love you," just one more time to him. we needed to create just one more memory with him. share one more meal with him. cry one more time with him.

but you knew like we knew, if you gave us one more time, we would always need

just one more time with him.

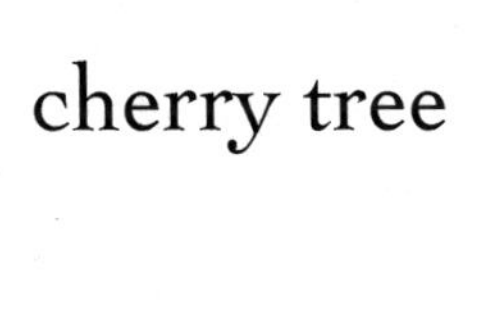

cherry tree

cherry trees gave springtime and new beginnings permission to arrive.

she knew because one grew in the backyard of her childhood home. she used to watch from the top bunk of the bed she shared with her sister, waiting for the cherries on the cherry tree to grow.

she waited throughout the seasons.
she watched the seasons come and go.
she watched winter rear its ugly storms into their backyard. blizzards, sometimes. so bad, you lost sight of the turquoise and blues that stood out from the play set.

she watched fall creep in, right after summer.
she watched as the trees wept because the leaves were falling and she watched when they came back in the spring; it was one of the most beautiful forms of love her young eyes had ever witnessed.

she had never taken her eyes off of the cherry tree.

the cherry tree kept daddy home.

they were filled with excitement: candy in a piñata waiting to burst open. there was trouble that brewed and set in the home. it seemed to happen more often than not but the cherry tree and the cherries that grew from it gave her hope that the tension that left the air thick and the arguing that kept her up at night wouldn't settle. wouldn't last. it gave her all of the hope she needed.

spring brought showers. spring watered their cherry tree. she watched as mother nature took its course and allowed the cherries to grow. daddy said they didn't need to water the tree because the rain did it for them. some days, when he wasn't looking, she would water it anyway. just to give mother nature help. she had already worked hard enough.

summer: the cherries were ready to be picked. they picked them together. the excitement and love they shared reciprocated around as the world laughed, bursting a confetti of colors through floral arrangements.

her hands and daddy's hands and mama's hands would intertwine like dhikr beads and the cherries were her prayers. every cherry she would rinse, she would pray for all of the good that surrounded them to last into the changing of the leaves. they would eat them one by one, dipping them in an ant pile of sugar.

sweet was their favorite flavor.

fall: hope died. love died. happiness died when the cherries stopped coming.

in my mother's house, pt. ii

one.

mama was beautiful.

not in the flowers and rainbows and butterflies type of way. mama was a poem. she grew from trauma; it fed her. it motivated her. trauma provided her with a sliver of hope that the broken hearts and the damaged self-esteem and the verbal beatings wouldn't last forever.

she was raised from experiences that not everyone survives. she was raised from the experiences that you go through. experiences that you grow through.

mama was from the broken and ruined and piss-smelling and hard-core, crooked corners and crooked cops and drug dealers and gang bangers and kids dancing through bursting water from fire hydrant summers, streets of bronx, new york.

mama used to be big smiles in easter dresses and curly afros that you couldn't pick through because her puerto rican hair was too thick. mama was from a village that raised and took care of and protected their children.

mama was every type of beautiful

and i had the pleasure of witnessing her survival.

two.

mama called the rain tears from heaven. every time it would rain she would order my sister and i to grab mason jars to capture the rain. it was our favorite thing to do. my sister and i would watch from our small bedroom window, pushing each other out of the way as the clouds roared together.

"move, i can't see."
"you don't know what you're looking for. since, i'm the oldest. i do."
"yes huh! yes i do! we're waiting for the clouds to color the sky grey."

we drank tears from heaven for days.

we drank it when mama wasn't cooking with it or when daddy wasn't pouring the water out to store the items that he collected.

daddy's items were one of his best-kept secrets; he never let us near them.

daddy collected everything. mama said it kept his mind off of our situation. that was all she said. daddy had a pantry in the basement where he would house his items. he lined the bottom of each jar with dandelions.

daddy had a section in the backyard where he forbade my sister and i to play in. his section was full of bright yellow dandelions. every time daddy picked some, it seemed like double would grow in their place.

after he lined the bottom, he dropped one item in and sealed it. daddy kept a rusted tooth from a fork, a penny that said 1900, a piece of paper with cursive words scribbled on them: *i loved you endlessly*. there were some items we could ask daddy about. but, not everything. i asked daddy where he found this stuff. he said he was drawn to all of the items in his pantry. he said that he found them when he would walk around the neighborhood or he spotted things on the road. he said that he never looked for these items, they came to him.

daddy showed me the first item he ever collected. he said it was outside of the hospital where i was born. he was pacing outside of the hospital and he spotted a newborn's shoe under the bench. he said it was odd that it was there. he picked it up, put it in his pocket and that is when his collection started.

daddy never let us in his pantry without him. he said we would break something or put his jars out of order.

one spring day, my sister and i were playing hide and go seek in the backyard. it was the first day in weeks that the weather was nice: no rain just shine.

we were tempted by laughter and the thrill of playing tag with the sunrays.

my sister buried her face in the bushes as her hands protected her from mosquitos attempting to extract honey from her cheeks.

she screamed a muffled "1....2...3..." which was my cue to search for a hiding place.

we did not have many options when it came to hiding in our backyard: there was the big tree and daddy's old car, where we stopped hiding because of the raccoon that made it home for its babies.

the big tree, that reminded us of grandma willow from pocahontas, would be the first place my sister would look so i dashed into the plants that stood behind the fence. "ready or not, here i come!"

i ducked down low to make sure she would not see me, hoping that my floral dress would blend in with my hiding grounds. my sister gave no advances to hint how close she was to finding me. one of her "hide and go seek" strategies was to play in silence.

it tricks your opponent. they never hear you coming.

she was quiet and i was quiet. i listened for the few fallen leaves on the ground to crumple under her feet or for her to break a twig in two.

it seemed like hours had passed. since my sister played in silence, i wasn't sure if she was still looking for me anymore. i played with a bud that had barely sprouted into a dandelion from the ground. i didn't want to remove it as it still had potential to be something beautiful. a shadow, almost like a cloud blocking the sun, fell over me and the bud that i had been irritating.

i looked up to see if it looked like rain and there daddy stood, right above me, staring down with disappointment in his eyes. if i hadn't realized it before, i realized now that i was sitting in daddy's garden that held his field of dandelions.

i was still fiddling with the bud refusing to look daddy in his eyes. he yanked me up by my dress and the bud came right along with me. i could feel it struggle in my hands, as if it was not ready to come out of the ground.

daddy was screaming but i didn't hear anything he said as i was focused on the bud that never got a chance to grow.

five.

mama told my sisters and i bedtime stories every night. our favorite one was about the chaos that took place in heaven when god would send too much rain.

angel one / another rain storm?! i mean, come on! the trees are as vibrant and green and tall as they're going to be. the grass blades are thick and strong and ready to be climbed on and explored through by the ladybugs. the flowers, god, the flowers are as beautiful as they've ever been. the colors are so bright, you can see them from up here. the colors are so bright, it's blocking the sun's shine.

angel two / the world may be okay for the rest of the year without rain.

god didn't say anything. she sat and listened.

god/ even though i have created this beautiful world and all of the beautiful people who exist and walk around this earth, there are so many things i'm limited to. i can't stop hearts from breaking. can't stop tragedies from happening. you know what comforts me more than anything? i find comfort in being able to help as much as i can. i find comfort in being able to provide rain to two beautiful girls who collect the rain for their mother. i find comfort knowing our supply is limitless while theirs is limited. i can see and hear and feel all things. i know the pain of a man who struggles to support his family and the pain of the woman who watches him struggle through it; who feels his struggle. providing rain is the least i could do.

mama, god's a woman?

mama would place a finger over her lips, softly telling my sister to shhhh. her eyes jolted to the open door. we sat in silence.

mama/ god is a woman. but it's our secret. people think it's impossible for a woman to have created the earth and all of the beauty that it carries. but, women were created as creators. we make lives. we make homes complete. everything we touch becomes beautiful just like the world. we were created in god's image. always remember that. and she always finds ways to protect you. she is always with you.

but, where mama?

mama/ she's here. right here.

mama pointed to her heart.

six.

some nights, i would witness mama in the kitchen filling the mason jars with tap water from the sink. i knew the jars that my sister and i filled were never enough but i still believed god sent as much as she could.

the electricity would occasionally be cut off, too.

when that happened, mama would make sure we had dinner and were ready for bed before the sunset.

she would set flashlights by our bed just in case we needed to get up to go to the bathroom in the middle of the night.

my sister and i loved having flashlights by our bed. when mama would close our bedroom door, we'd light up the ceiling and make gestures with our fingers. we would giggle at how big our fingers looked on our stage.

i would know when my sister was asleep. her fingers would no longer make puppets on the ceiling and her light would be stuck in the corner of the room.

are you awake, i would ask knowing she wasn't.

mmmhmm. i'm up.

"jake, we only needed the water for a few days. just until the water bill was paid. i thought there were enough jars for what you needed."

daddy didn't say anything right away. his jaw muscles tightened as his eyes shifted between my sister, my mama and me.

for once it looked like he would let this one go.

everything moved in slow motion: his hand to her face.

there was speed in which everything registered.

i demanded my sister to run to the closet.

that was the first time we witnessed him hit mama.

he jabbed her with words that i knew i would never be able to speak in anger to anyone.

i didn't even want to think about the words he was saying because mama always told me god hears and sees everything and i didn't want god mad at me.

i ended up in the closet with my sister. i sat next to her cupping my hands over her ears. as best as i could, i wanted to drown out the obscenities both my parents were fetching at each other, away from her. my sister was younger than me but she was able to understand that the situation was a bad one and she was always so concerned about mama.

there wasn't much i could do to protect her especially since i had no control over any of my parents fights but i tried… i tried hard.

it rained that night… was god sending tears, again? i guess she knew ours were all dried out.

eight.

there was a moment that i witnessed and i could tell daddy might love mama but mama never showed it back.

daddy had days where he would be in a good mood and he only wanted to be around mama. he would pull her on his lap while he was watching television and shower her with kisses and tickles but mama rarely laughed or smiled.

this was the only time she could be stern with him and he wouldn't get mad. he thought mama's rejection was cute and it would make him want to love on her more.

these were the moments that i loved and i wished that mama would accept them.

daddy's smile was perfect and white and when he showed it, it would light up the room. daddy was beautiful when he smiled.

nine.

love collected dust on the mantle. our home was the first space i learned of the inauthenticity of love. i learned that love could be present but it could feel forced. i learned that love could feel like an obligation. i learned that love could be broken. and ruined. and uncomfortable. and filled with pain. and regret. i learned that love could make you feel good. and that it could make you feel bad. i learned love could make you howl curses to the moon; the moon was the only one awake. the only one who would listen to you. i learned that love could hurt and it could hurt deep; it could cut deep. i learned that there was nothing that could stitch the wound back together. i learned that even if the wound scabs over, the memory of the heartbreak and the trauma… it forever remains.

i learned that love could be lonely.

and empty. even when it was sharing space with you.

love could feel empty even when it was sitting right next to you.

the wind blew chills outside but it had not rained that day.

daddy stumbled in drunk on his 35th birthday.

it wasn't something that was new to us but usually my sister and i would be in bed by the time he returned.

i occupied the one bathroom in the house, stuffing my training bra to see how much tissue i needed to make my breasts look natural like the other more developed 13-year-olds at school.

when i heard daddy's voice, fear struck and a sense of urgency rushed through my body as i removed the tissue from my bra and buried them in the trashcan.

quietly, i opened the bathroom door and tiptoed into me and my sisters' room, which was right by the bathroom. i climbed into the top bunk and closed my eyes just in case daddy came in to check on us.

instead of allowing time to make sure we were in bed, mama confronted him about coming home so late. we could hear her, at least i could, and this time mama wasn't calm.

which one were you with tonight?

mama's voice shivered as she tried to maintain her anger.

i knew mama had to be afraid because i was afraid for her. i wondered what it was that made mama believe that daddy had been with other women.

i was able to catch bits and pieces of the argument that night.

go ba-back to bed, daddy said. his words stumbling over each other.

no! no! who were you with?

i had never heard mama raise her voice at daddy and it terrified me.

be-bed. go to bed.

why do you do this?! why do you do this to us?! why don't you love me?

why don't you love me…

i've been good to you…

i cook. i clean.

i try not to question you.

i try to love you.

i try to love you.

but you won't let me love you.

mama's cries and the tears that raced down my cheek lulled me to sleep.

the tension was thick the mornings and days and nights after mama and daddy's argument. by the third day, i convinced my sister to walk to the store with me.

we lived in a small town. when we were allowed, we loved walking to the small store in town. we loved watching and listening to the people who occupied the store frequently.

we saw mrs. jean and mrs. salem down the frozen food aisle.

these women claimed they were mama's friends but i heard them gossip about her on a number of occasions.

"bet'chu they mama got that battered woman disease," said mrs. jean looking over her shoulder and through her glasses at my sister and i.

i pretended to be occupied in looking for vegetables but i could hear them loud and clear.

"what'chu talkin' bout battered woman disease?"

"you know exactly what i'm talkin' bout. that woman in there gettin' beat and has no desire to leave."

"you don't know that. maybe she scared."

scared? that's exactly what mama was.

the women in the grocery store continued talking like my sister and i weren't there. these same women were the women who were sitting at our dining room table some days when my sister and i came home from school, laughing and chatting with mama.

there was even one time when i came home from school and it looked as if mama had been crying to mrs. jean.

but on that day, at the grocery store, both of them acted like they didn't even know us. they acted like they had never been mama's friends. mama always told us we couldn't trust everybody. she told us that all we had was each other. i was starting to see that now.

it was going on five years since i had been home and nothing changed about mama's house; except it looked bigger than i remembered.

she moved into this small house after she separated from daddy.

i only spent a year of my life in it.

the window on the second floor hung by the hinges. it reminded me of a drooping eye that always looked down at the feet of its owner. never looking anyone in their eyes as if afraid of what everyone else may think.

the house lacked confidence.

it reminded me of mama: small with stairwells as narrow as her hips.

mama carried memories inside of her like the house did; memories that she would never share with anyone. i attempted to convince my siblings that the weight of those memories are what killed mama.

they called me insane for thinking up such a thing

my sister, racine, was too young when the relationship was really bad between mama and daddy so she was going to believe what she was told.

her belief leaned a lot more towards my sister, cleo's memory. she could not fathom the idea of daddy being a man she had never known him to be.

i always thought cleo was old enough to remember.

she chose to erase the man who raised us from her memory and she re-created him. i'm not sure if i was upset that she refused to remember who he was or if i was upset because i wished that i could re-create him, too.

racine said she remembered when daddy had money and showered us with gifts. she remembered when daddy tried to move mama out of the house and into something bigger.

daddy changed when mama divorced him. he carried remorse and regret.

he tried his best to make sure that we would always remember him as a good father. but, i could never allow myself to forget what he did to mama.

those memories were stored in a special part of my brain that no one had access to. sort of like daddy's dandelion lined mason jars.

fourteen.

i overheard mama saying that daddy loved women. she made it sound like it was something beyond his control. like it was something she had no choice but to understand.

i knew she was hurt. the hurt was laced in the passages of her throat and came out every time she talked about daddy and his women. it was laced in her voice; this hurt.

daddy didn't pack his belongings or his apologies or his regrets. he left them out lingering.

he convinced mama that we would not be able to get by without him and that he had to stay for us. so, mama accepted it.

when mama got a part time job, daddy would bring the women to the house. he left them in the kitchen and told me and my sister we couldn't go in there.

we wouldn't. but i would pass by. i always wanted to get a glimpse of them. i was always curious if he was interested in women who looked like mama.

i always thought they were beautiful and i felt like i shouldn't have. i felt like i was betraying my mama for thinking such things.

and then mama would come home, even after the women were long gone and an argument would happen. it was almost as if she knew.

i watched a television show about a woman's intuition.

i didn't think all women had it but i was convinced that mama did.

fifteen.

mama's house was cold; it reminded me of the way she existed on this earth.

i was at mama's bedside the day she passed away; everything happened so suddenly.

she called me one day and asked if i could stop by because she wasn't feeling well and by the next day, she was dying.

my hands were cupped around her frozen hands trying to keep her warm but it didn't work. i couldn't understand why her body was so cold.

she shivered for hours, a pile of blankets stacked on top of her.

i told her a story about how god and her angels were waiting for her to return to them. i told her that my sisters and i would be okay. i told her that god placed a shield of protection around us and within the shield, we had each other. i told her the rivers in heaven flowed with milk and honey that would nurture her soul every day. i told her she would walk barefoot on clouds. i told her that her heart would beat vibrantly again. i told her that she would never be alone again.

she would never be broken again.
she would be loved.
and appreciated.

mama's face smiled: her eyes shimmered like the stars and the corners of her lips rose like the sun.

"i'm going to run to the funeral home and make final arrangements. anyone want to come with?"

my sisters declined.

they insisted on staying behind and packing up mama's belongings.

i exited the entryway and someone on the outside stopped right at the door. it didn't look as if they planned on ringing the bell; it almost looked as if they were contemplating being there at all.

we didn't say anything to each other right away when i opened the door. we just stared.

the heavy bags that rested under his eyes and the wrinkles that produced on his forehead were proof that in the last five years that i hadn't seen him, life had begun taking its toll.

he still dressed sharp; just like he did when i was a teenager.

he helped establish a transportation company in our town. the neighborhood kids used to say he dressed so nice that he could walk down the street and be hired anywhere, on the spot.

we stayed in our cramped home until i graduated because mama said there was no reason to start somewhere new if we were going to bring the old with us.

there was a reason why silence was so awkward: it left an empty space for words that you were too ashamed or too proud to say.

my father and i were stubborn in the same sense: i was standing there waiting for him to speak as he was standing there waiting for me.

although stubborn, he was still the man that i once thought was beautiful when he smiled.

a smirk spread across his face and the beautiful white smile of his that i loved so much peeked through.

"it's good to see you, daddy."

i did not give him a chance to speak.

i walked pass him and heard him mumble something under his breath but i didn't bother to find out what.

i proceeded to my car, hands in my pocket and i felt a raindrop tap my nose: tears from heaven.

"In the end, your past is not my past and your truth is not my truth and your solution - is not my solution."
– Zadie Smith

Made in the USA
Lexington, KY
04 July 2017